Take-Off! **What are ...?**
ISLANDS

Claire Llewellyn

Heinemann
LIBRARY

www.heinemann.co.uk
Visit our website to find out more information about Heinemann Library books.

To order:

☎ Phone 44 (0) 1865 888066

 Send a fax to 44 (0) 1865 314091

 Visit the Heinemann Bookshop at www.heinemann.co.uk to browse our catalogue and order online.

First published in Great Britain by Heinemann Library,
Halley Court, Jordan Hill, Oxford OX2 8EJ,
a division of Reed Educational and Professional Publishing Ltd.
Heinemann is a registered trademark of Reed Educational and Professional Publishing Ltd.

OXFORD MELBOURNE AUCKLAND
JOHANNESBURG BLANTYRE GABORONE
IBADAN PORTSMOUTH (NH) USA CHICAGO

Designed by David Oakley
Illustrated by Hardlines and Jo Brooker
Originated by Dot Gradations
Printed by South China Printing in Hong Kong/China

ISBN 0 431 02441 3 (hardback)   ISBN 0 431 02446 4 (paperback)
05 04 03 02 01   05 04 03 02 01
10 9 8 7 6 5 4 3 2 1   10 9 8 7 6 5 4 3 2 1

British Library Cataloguing in Publication Data

Llewellyn, Claire
  What are islands?. – (Take-off!)
  1.Islands – Juvenile literature
  I.Title II.Islands
  551.4'2

Acknowledgements

The publishers would like to thank the following for permission to reproduce photographs: Ecoscene: Alan Towse p.19; FLPA: S Jonasson p.11, Ian Cartwright p.12, Silvestris p.13, E&D Hosking p.14; NASA: Johnson Space Centre p.22, p.24, p.26; Oxford Scientific Films: Scott Winer p.4, W Gregory Brown p.5, W Johnson p.10, Stan Osolonski p.16, Frances Furlong/Survival Anglia p.29; Robert Harding Picture Library: Robert Francis p.6; Still Pictures: Yves Thonnerieux p.17, DRA p.20, B&C Alexander p.28; Telegraph Colour Library: Chris Mellor p.7; Trip: W Jacobs p.15, S Grant p.18, C Rennie p.21.

Cover photograph reproduced with permission of Oxford Scientific Films/Scott Winer.

Our thanks to Sue Graves and Hilda Reed for their advice and expertise in the preparation of this book.

Every effort has been made to contact copyright holders of any material reproduced in this book. Any omissions will be rectified in subsequent printings if notice is given to the publishers.

Contents

Any words appearing in the text in bold, **like this**, are explained in the Glossary.

What is an island?

An island is a piece of land surrounded by water.
It may be in a river, a lake or the sea.

island

sand

sea

The sea surrounds this island.

sea   shallow water   islands

These islands are so small that nobody lives on them.

Some islands are huge, and some are home to millions of people. But most islands are very small. They often lie in groups in the sea.

The largest island in the world is Greenland. It has an area of about 2,175,000 square kilometres.

Cut off by water

Some islands, like the British Isles, were once joined to larger pieces of land called **continents**. They were cut off when the **sea level** rose.

British coast

ferry

sea

Many people like to take the ferry from Britain to reach the continent of Europe.

The mainland of Great Britain is the eighth largest island in the world.

St Michael's Mount

low tide

People can only reach St Michael's Mount when the tide is low.

Some pieces of land, like St Michael's Mount in the UK, are islands only at high **tide**. People can walk to the islands when the tide is low.

How are islands made?

Madagascar was once part of the continent of Africa.

Some islands are made when a piece of land breaks away from a **continent**. The two pieces slowly drift apart.

Madagascar is about 400 km from the coast of Africa.

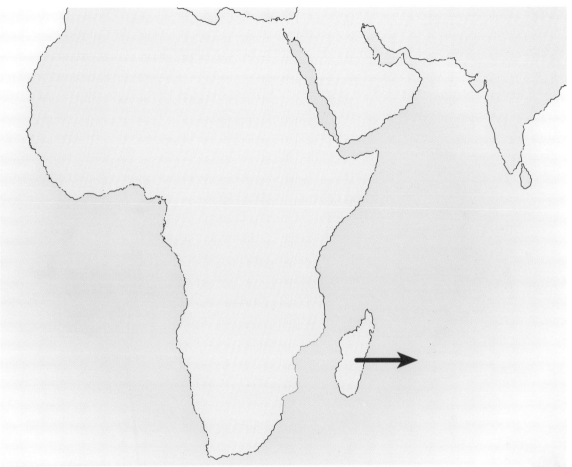

When the Earth's surface moved, the land became surrounded by sea.

Fifty million years ago, a huge piece of land broke away from the continent of Africa. The land became surrounded by sea. This land became the island of Madagascar.

Volcanoes in the sea

Other islands are the tops of **volcanoes** on the sea-bed. When a volcano **erupts**, hot **lava** pours out and piles up around it. Slowly, the volcano grows bigger.

islands

sea

These islands are the tops of volcanoes that erupted under the sea.

Volcanic islands like Japan were made when underwater volcanoes erupted. Find Japan on a world map.

After thousands of years, some undersea volcanoes grow so tall that they reach the surface. They stick out of the sea. This makes new islands.

Surtsey Island

crater

This 'new' island, called Surtsey, appeared near Iceland in 1963.

The island was named Surtsey after Surtur, the Norse god of fire.

Coral islands

Tiny animals called corals live in the sea and make rock-like **reefs**. Over many thousands of years, the reefs pile up to make islands.

Coral reefs are made by billions of tiny animals called corals.

coral

fish

The longest reef in the world is the Great Barrier Reef off the coast of north-eastern Australia. It stretches for 2027 km.

Coral islands are sometimes shaped like a ring. They lie very low in the water and are often flooded in storms.

island

sea

This ring-shaped island lies low in the water.

A coral island in the shape of a ring is called an atoll.

New island life

There are no plants or animals on a new island. As time passes, birds fly to the island. Other animals swim there or float on logs.

island

Nothing lives or grows on this island at the moment.

plants

bird

Seeds grow into plants on new islands and birds come to feed and nest on them.

Seeds are blown to the new island or are washed up by the sea. They start to grow in the sand.

Look again at the picture on page 11 of Surtsey appearing in 1963. By 1980, there was a whole breeding colony of sea birds on the island!

Island animals

penguin

Galapagos penguins are not used to people. They have no fear of them.

Many islands are far from the nearest land. The animals on the islands have never been hunted by other animals or by people.

Some island animals live nowhere else in the world. This can make them very rare.

giant tortoise

This giant tortoise is very rare. It is only found on the Galapagos Islands.

The Galapagos Islands are in the Pacific Ocean and are about 800 km from the mainland!

Away from it all

Many islands are quiet places. They are far from cities, motorways and modern life, so they are good places for wildlife.

sea

pelican

This island in Florida is a safe place for pelicans to raise their young.

rock

island   hotels

Many people enjoy taking their holidays
on these islands near Australia.

Many people enjoy taking their holidays on islands.
This brings jobs to the islands because visitors need
hotels and restaurants. But extra people and
buildings can damage the islands and their wildlife.

19

Living on islands

Some countries are made up of islands. Japan is made up of 3900 islands, but most people live on the four biggest islands.

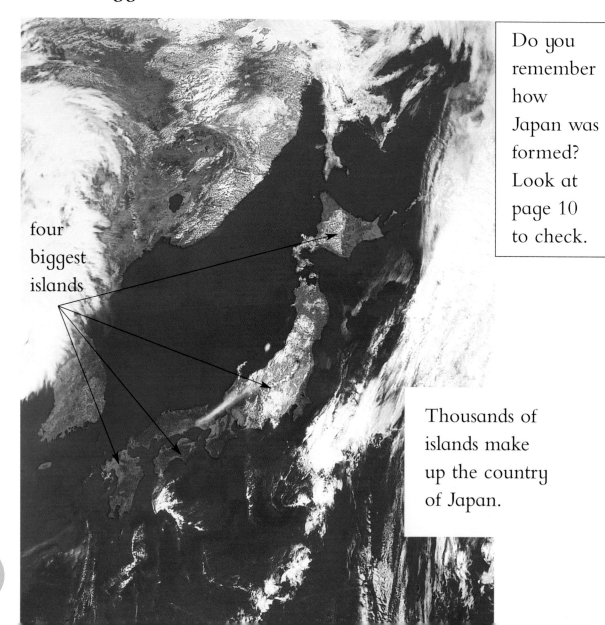

four biggest islands

Do you remember how Japan was formed? Look at page 10 to check.

Thousands of islands make up the country of Japan.

People travel between Japan's islands on this train. It is called the 'bullet train'. Can you guess why?

Long bridges and tunnels have been built between the islands of Japan. People and goods can reach every part of the country.

Island map 1

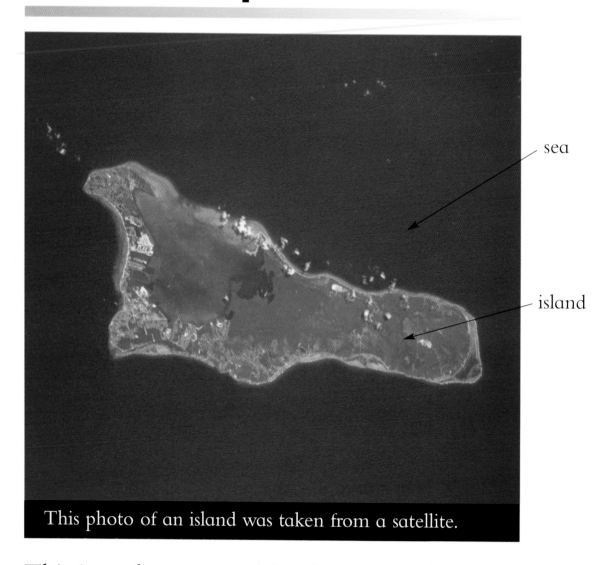

sea

island

This photo of an island was taken from a satellite.

This is a photo of an island. It was taken from a **satellite**. The island is surrounded by the sea.

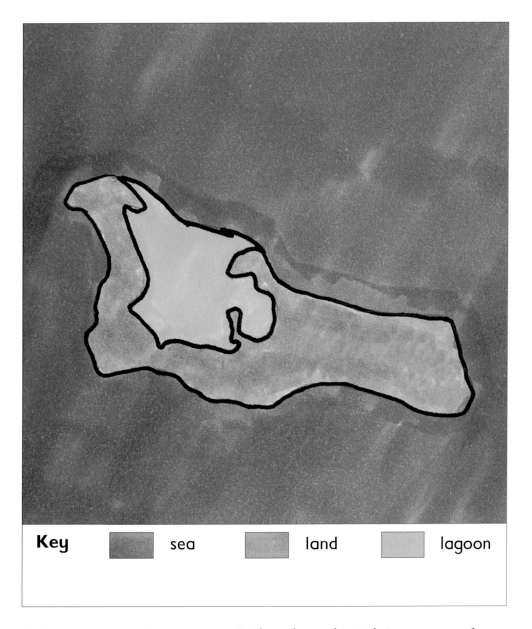

Maps are pictures of the land. This map shows us the same place as the photo. The key tells us what each colour means.

Island map 2

beach

buildings

coral reef

You can see buildings, beaches and coral reefs on this bigger photo.

The same island looks bigger in this photo. You can see that there are buildings on some parts of the island. There are beaches and coral **reefs** around the shore.

24

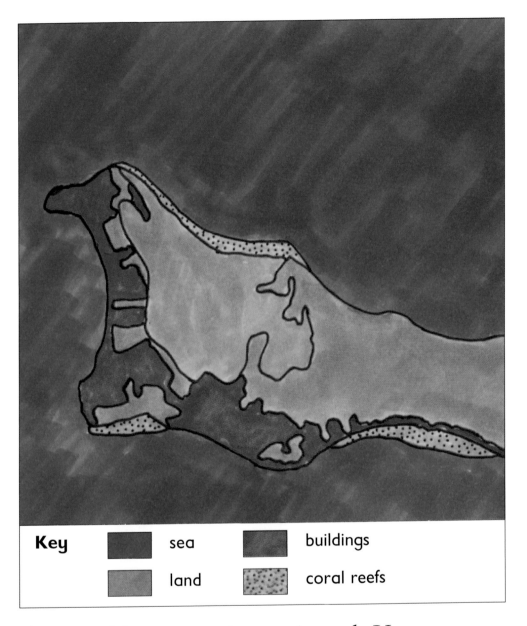

Key

▨ sea	▨ buildings
▨ land	▨ coral reefs

The buildings are shown in red. You can see that there are very few buildings in the middle of the island. Most of them are along the shore. Look at the key to help you find the coral reefs.

Island map 3

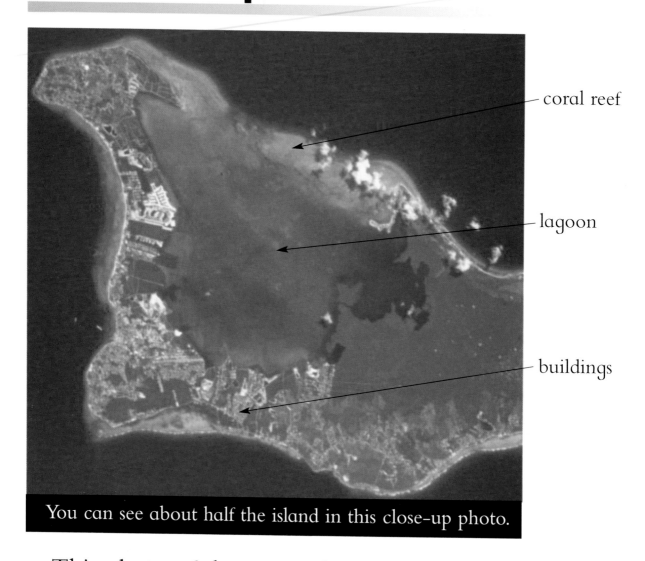

coral reef

lagoon

buildings

You can see about half the island in this close-up photo.

This photo of the same island is even closer. You can see about half the island. You can see buildings and roads around the edges of the island. At the top of the island is a large **lagoon**.

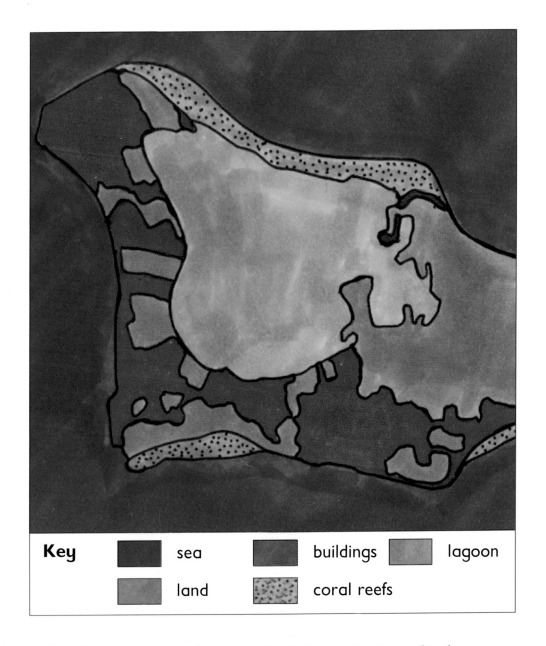

Key

■	sea	■	buildings	■	lagoon
■	land	▦	coral reefs		

The lagoon is shown in blue. It is a lighter blue than the sea because the water is shallower here.

Amazing island facts

Greenland is the world's largest island. It is six times bigger than Germany but its population is one thousand times smaller. Most of Greenland is covered with thick sheets of ice.

Greenland is the largest island in the world.

Tristan da Cunha is a very remote island.

Tristan de Cunha is the world's most **remote** island. It is home to about 200 people. They live 2740 kilometres from the nearest **continent** – that's a five-hour journey by plane.

Tristan da Cunha lies in the South Atlantic.

Glossary

a b c d e f g h i j k l m n o p q r s t u v w x y z

continent a very large piece of land. There are seven continents on Earth.

erupt suddenly shoot out lava and ash from deep inside the Earth

lagoon sheltered shallow water that lies behind a coral reef

lava hot rock that shoots out of a volcano

reef tiny animals called corals live in the sea. Their skeletons build up to make reefs.

remote far away from anything or anywhere else

satellite a special machine that goes around the Earth in space. It can take photographs of the Earth.

sea level the usual level of the sea

tide the level that the sea goes up and down each day

volcano mountain made out of lava. It sometimes erupts, shooting out hot rock and ash from inside the Earth.

More books to read

Nicola Baxter.
Our Wonderful Earth.
Two-Can, 1997

Claire Llewellyn.
What Are...Coral Reefs?
Heinemann Library, 2001

Rosanne Hooper and Monica Byles.
Islands.
Two-Can, 1992

Terry Jennings.
Our Earth: Coasts and Islands.
Belitha Press, 1989

Index